CONTENTS

	Introduction: Why Write A Parent's Guide?	6
1	The Challenge of Defeating the Bully	8
2	What Every Parent Needs to Know About Bullying	10
3	Understanding the Roots of Bullying	12
4	Why Bullying Could Be the Best Thing That Could Happen to Your Children	14
5	The Many Faces of Bullying	17
6	Information Gathering: The Most Often Missed Step in Helping Your Children Deal with the Bully	21
7	Teach Your Child an Effective Communications Strategy	24
8	Three Easy Skills Your Child Must Know to Keep Safe	27
9	Parent Communication with the School	34
10	Communication with the Bully's Parents	37
11	Frequently Asked Questions	39
12	Final Thoughts and Additional Resources	45
	About the Author, Christopher Rappold	47

INTRODUCTION
WHY WRITE A PARENT'S GUIDE?

As a teacher of a character-based martial arts program since 1991, I have seen firsthand the debilitating effects of bullying in the lives of too many children:

• A child who was happy and well-adjusted at school was suddenly shut down and had their potential stifled as a result of the presence of a bully;

• A child who went from A's and B's and loving school to failing and not wanting to go to class, all the result of a bully;

• Fathers and mothers who sat in my office with tear-filled eyes trying to find the answers for what to do because their child is being harassed at school.

As a result of these experiences, I was compelled to write this book as a way of providing much needed guidance and support that I truly believe will provide families with a solution-based roadmap.

When a child is guided correctly to deal strategically with a bully, he will grow up differently. The situation will become a springboard instead of a cliff. They feel empowered instead of fearful. They learn that conflict is inevitable, but dealing correctly with conflict doesn't have to be a roadblock – just a temporary detour to navigate around.

Parents who use these skills to educate their children will find a bright light at the end of what sometimes feels like a dark tunnel. I am happy and proud to be part of the solution that will allow your child to realize their Personal Best.

All the Best,

Christopher Rappold

5-Time World Karate Champion

Founder

Personal Best Karate

Child Safety Consultant

Norton, Massachusetts

1. THE CHALLENGE OF DEFEATING THE BULLY

*As parents, one of our highest responsibilities is
to ensure that our children meet their challenges with
an intelligent plan and the psychology to overcome
their fears, doubts and worries.*

If you could make a choice between ridding the world of
bullies *or* learning the mindset and skills to minimize or eliminate
their negative impact on your child, which would you choose?

Think about it carefully because your answer to the question
will reveal how you view the challenge before you. At times,
parents can feel powerless against the never- ending siege of
negative experiences from which we cannot protect our children. It
can be painful to be a spectator to your child's struggles with a
bully. Haven't you wished that the bully would just "go away" so
your son or daughter could happily continue down life's path? Has
it ever really happened? Sure, occasionally you will have the rare
treat of having the bully moving out of the state, but how often
does that occur? When it does, everyone breathes a sigh of relief.
Unfortunately, it is only a matter of time before the same challenge
rears its ugly head again.

In life we will have challenges put before us. When we face
them, we can expand our capacity to take on other challenges.
When we do not face our challenges, the same challenge will
continue to appear until we either face it and grow or make

ourselves smaller in attempts to win by avoidance.

When children choose to become smaller, they turn inward, become withdrawn, stop taking risks and limit their capacity to learn and enjoy life.

It's not a good place to be.

Defeating the bully is really about defeating your and your child's fears, doubts and worries. It is less about the person and more about you than you may realize… and this is great news.

When it's about us, we can take control of it.

It becomes infinitely harder when we are trying to control someone else's behavior. The real challenge of defeating the bully is the realization that the fight is with us and not with the offender. When we take this approach, regardless of the tactics the bully uses, we will minimize, if not completely eliminate, his or her negative effects.

2. WHAT EVERY PARENT NEEDS TO KNOW ABOUT BULLYING

Challenge and adversity brought by an adversary is what brings out the hidden potential in your child.

Bullying may be the greatest gift your son or daughter will receive this year. I realize this is a bold statement, especially if you find yourself currently in the thick of an emotional battle, but trust me… it can be true.

The makeup of every fairytale with which your child is familiar feature a peaceful setting, disrupted by a "bully" who attempts to take control of something or someone. Confusion and chaos follow until at long last the "hero" has a realization that sets him free to defeat the bully.

In fact, the formula for most fairy tales is:

Peace and Harmony + Bully = Chaos and Confusion

Chaos and Confusion / New Realization = Peace and Harmony

If the formula is so predictable and simple, then why don't children simply gravitate to this? The reason may be because children are so caught up in the far-off land, the dragon, the sword fights and other "entertaining" attributes put into the tale that they miss the message of how it relates to them.

As a parent, here is the really exciting point to understand. In most cases, the missing realization causing the chaos and confusion was undiscovered within the hero, until the "bully" set it free. Without the "bully" we may not have had *The Lion King*. Challenge and adversity brought by an adversary is what brings out the hidden potential in your child. In a world without challenge and adversity there is little growth.

Parents at times can exacerbate the problem by allowing their emotions to skyrocket out of control when they hear an offense was made towards their child. They get upset, their child sees them getting upset, and now "turbo chaos" has been created.

When you as a parent see bullying as a chance to grow, your emotions are kept in a productive range, and you will significantly help your child by learning the skills that will be covered in the next chapters.

3. UNDERSTANDING THE ROOTS OF BULLYING

Sometimes it's easy to forget that the child who is causing the hurt is probably hurting, too.

When someone with a chronic headache goes to see a medical doctor, chances are high that the physician will prescribe a drug that has a great chance of alleviating the pain. Problem solved... right? Maybe, but it's not hard to figure out why this approach is so popular: with the reduction of the headache, the patient feels relief and often thinks that he is cured.

When a patient goes to see a doctor of Chinese Medicine, the doctor provides a thorough examination, not to alleviate the pain but rather to see what is *causing* the pain. When the "root' cause is discovered, the doctor attempts to extinguish it. Since the body is so interconnected, the headache could be caused by a problem that originates in the person's foot, a diagnosis that would be missed with the traditional medical approach.

Both approaches may work; however, when we take the time to understand the root, we have a greater chance of keeping the symptoms from recurring.

How does this relate to bullying and why is understanding its root cause so important? Sometimes it's easy to forget that the child causing the hurt is probably hurting, too.

Where do bullies come from?

Broken homes and/or homes that lack solid parental

supervision and support may lead to the creation of bullies. They are children crying out for something to be cured within them and they act out their own hurt in unpopular ways. Often they lack the basic social skills for creating friendships in their lives; they live with the need to get attention the wrong way, because in their minds, negative attention is better than no attention at all.

While all children will go through small versions of these feelings, children who truly come from the background described above are destined to live there forever, unless something changes for them.

The truth is that bullies aren't people to fear, but rather people whom we should feel badly for. As parents, it's important to think of this first before you shout out marching orders to your child or make demands that the bully is never to be within 25 feet of your child at school. When a child makes a cry for help, it's the responsibility of the adults around to support the child the best way they can. Also, keep in mind that by removing the bully from your child you have not helped your child learn the skills and the mindset to successfully deal with the next bully that comes along.

4. WHY BULLYING MAY BE THE BEST THING THAT COULD HAPPEN TO YOUR CHILD

The challenge is not with the bully, the challenge is the reaction of the child who exposes his/her readiness to handle pushback.

When I look back on my years at school and think about the teachers I had, I have an adult realization: some of my toughest teachers taught me the most. Though I didn't like the extra homework, additional assignments and hours of reading, they forced me to do something I wouldn't have otherwise done myself … push myself.

When children come from a home that provides love, support and structure, they feel as if they have control of the world and their environment.

When they get on the school bus and start to meet other kids who don't share that same love of them, oftentimes they don't know how to handle the verbal harassment or the unwelcoming look that says, "find another seat".

These experiences of bullying may be the best thing that could happen to your child. The reason is simple. Perhaps for the first time, your child comes face to face with someone outside of their protected environment who doesn't show the same level of caring they are used to receiving. In most cases, what immediately follows is the hurt feeling and the tears when they arrive home from school, sharing with you the "horrors" of the day.

Your child is experiencing typical age-appropriate pushback. What creates the "horror" is that this is their first go-round with someone treating them this way.

Get on almost any city bus in America and, as adults, you will experience many unwelcome looks and stares that tell you to find another seat. In fact, depending on the city you're in, you might get more than that. Why is this not bothersome to adults? Because we understand that this is part of life, we keep a healthy perspective and find another seat.

Part of the experience for your child is a test of their confidence. When something negative happens to a confident child, they accept it and move on. When something happens to a child that is timid, they may see it as the end of the world. The point is that the challenge is not with the bully. The challenge is the reaction of the child who exposes their readiness to handle pushback.

Without this experience, you would only be able to hazard a guess at your child's ability to handle this. Now you know where he/she stands in a situation of pushback.

Here are three simple steps to immediately begin addressing this challenge:

1. Take the time to discuss what happened with your child.

As you're doing this, be aware of your reaction; it will either calm or intensify your child's perception of the event. The idea is to allow them the exercise of expressing their feelings, a skill set that, in and of itself, will be valuable to them.

2. Remind them that they are loved and respect their feelings.

When you are feeling great, you know you are loved, cared for and that you are important; everything else around you tends to be kept in perspective. When the world doesn't cooperate with you as in the bus example, it's a small annoyance as opposed to a day-wrecking event. Perspective is the order of the day, and keeping it reinforces healthy reaction.

3. Let them know that what happened is not personal against them and that their reaction to the pushback is more important than getting a seat.

Why? Because this is the seed of repeated psychological bullying. When the bully and everyone on the bus see what happened, they gain insight into how they can and cannot treat your child. They are unconsciously making judgments on who will be an easy future target.

The most important takeaway for you as a parent is that you have an opportunity to rate your child on a scale of 1 to 10 on their ability to handle this scenario. Armed with that knowledge, your goal is to improve their ability to handle this or similar situations.

Because of this pushback, you will not have to guess anymore about your child's ability to handle these types of situations. You are now on the road to building your child's resistance to the acts of bullying.

5. THE MANY FACES OF BULLYING

Statistics indicate that 97% of the time bullying occurs without the use of someone being touched. It's the words and poor treatment that makes up the majority of incidences.

Bullying takes many forms. It can be a threat, making fun of someone or simply excluding them from group activities. It can be mean-spirited or distant and cold. It can be one-on-one or it can spread to situations where a group of students are all focusing negative energy on one lone soul. Whatever the exact description, it is *all* considered bullying.

Many of these infractions committed one time may simply be rude or considered bad manners. When something is done repeatedly and it is clear the person is doing the act intentionally with the outcome to cause emotional harm, the offense can be accurately defined as bullying.

Typically, when someone envisions bullying, what immediately comes to mind is the scene of a timid boy being pushed on the playground. While that definitely qualifies as bullying, physical confrontation makes up a small amount of the instances. Statistics indicate that 97% of the time bullying occurs without the use of someone being touched. It's the words and poor treatment that makes up the majority of incidences. In fact, one could argue that verbal harassment is much more damaging long-term than physical harm.

Two children agree to fight physically: one wins and one gets a black eye. In a few days the eye heals and life goes on. However, when someone is verbally harassed, the negative words and feelings can linger on for years. Haven't you ever seen adults who continue running the same pattern of self-limiting beliefs that they probably learned early in life? Make no mistake about it, words hurt!

The bottom line is that bullying comes in many forms and that whatever the tactics, it can be very damaging to someone's self-esteem or their personal happiness.

Here's a list of the many faces that bullying behavior can take:

Attention-getter: A person who continually seeks attention at the expense of others.

Beggar: A person who continually demands what others have.

Blackmailer: A person who continually uses the threat of unpleasant consequences to get what they want.

Braggart: A person who continually uses their accomplishments to make others feel inferior.

Caller-outer: A person who continually challenges those around them.

Conversation hog: A person who continually talks and monopolizes time, preventing others from having their fair share of a discussion.

Copycat:A person who continually imitates what another does.

Criticizer: A person who continually emphasizes the negatives in another person or situation.

Destroyer: A person who continually disrupts the peace and harmony of a situation.

Disrespecter: A person who continually treats others in a way that doesn't pay them appropriate respect.

Distracter: A person who continually attempts to break the concentration and focus of others through words and actions.

Humiliator: A person who continually attempts to embarrass others through the use of words or actions.

Interrupter: A person who continually invades conversations and games without any thought for the other people's feelings.

Liar: A person who continually engages in dishonesty, and uses untruths to get what they want.

Name-caller: A person who repeats an unflattering or tone of a name for the purpose of annoying others.

Pusher/shover: A person who continually uses physical contact to annoy or intimidate others.

Rumor spreader: A person who continually engages in spreading truths or untruths that the victim would not want repeated.

Show-off: A person who continually attempts to use their superior skill or knowledge in a way to make others feel badly.

Snooper/spyer: A person who continuously tries to find out what others are doing; someone with little regard for the personal privacy of others.

Space Invader: A person who continually gets physically closer than what others wants or feel comfortable with.

Stalker: A person who continually follows others wherever they go on the playground or within a classroom.

Tattletale: A person who continually reports someone for the simple pleasure of seeing that person gets in trouble.

Teaser: A person who continually finds a weakness in others – either real or perceived – and continually harasses the person by calling out the weakness.

Thief: A person who continually steals the property of others.

Trash-talker: Originated and popularized in sports, a trash-talker uses disrespectful or "putdown" language to make an opponent feel intimidated.

Whiner: A person who continually engages in the behavior of complaining about perceived injustices.

6. INFORMATION GATHERING: THE MOST OFTEN MISSED STEP IN HELPING YOUR CHILD DEAL WITH THE BULLY

You, more than anyone in the world,
will have the greatest impact upon
your child's growth and development

It is an awesome responsibility and an equally awesome opportunity, especially when things in your child's life do not go well.

When children are given what feels like more than they can emotionally handle, instantly, they turn to you. This is great, because when they turn to you, it provides you the opportunity to help shape the way they respond. By staying calm and listening to them, you will show them (non-verbally) that what feels like the end of the world to them is only their perception. This is a great start. Remember, communication is 70% physiology; the way you show caring and compassion for their feelings tied together with calmness teaches them that they too can be calm in the face of challenge.

Allow your child to share all of their feelings, thoughts and emotions about what happened. Allow them to talk and share their feelings without judgment. This may take five minutes or it may take a period of venting followed by a bike ride or some television –whatever helps your child release their grip on a traumatic event of the day. After you sense that the walls are down and your child has enjoyed a much needed emotional release, gently start asking questions to get the exact sequence of events, including who was involved and specifically what each person did. The clearer a picture you can get from them, the better you will be able to help.

You must go through an information-gathering step first. Often what parents do is make the mistake of immediately acting when all the facts aren't yet known. Also, by verbalizing the scenario, it helps to drain your child's emotions. Isn't it true that we always feel better when we have a chance to talk it out? Let the air out of the balloon and you will find that your child will be much more receptive to your feedback.

Here is a list of questions that I have found helpful when trying to sift through the challenge:

Can you tell me *specifically* what happened?

The key word is "specifically." Emotional children will talk in general terms saying things like, "I got milk thrown at me at lunchtime" when what really may have happened is someone accidentally spilled milk that ended up running off the table onto them and the child next to them laughed.

Can you tell me the *exact* order of how this happened?

If you saw the movie *Apollo 13,* you will remember that the sequence of how they "powered up" the equipment was vital to their being able to get back to Earth. If they did one step out of order, they would have wasted valuable electrical power that would have prevented the safe return of the astronauts. In the same manner, sequencing in-school bullying is extremely valuable to establish a timeline of the occurrence. Often you will find that if your child acted differently, they may have prevented an escalation. Without knowing this precisely, it will be impossible to create "Best Responses."

Can you tell me *specifically* who was involved?

Again, the key word is "specifically." Emotional children will say things like "everyone was laughing at me" when really there were only two people who were laughing. It's also a valuable exercise for your child to make an informal study of how others react when something happens. Who are the laughers? Who are the students who ran to get a teacher? Who are the people who just stood around and watched? Who were the students who stepped in and tried to make peace?

What was *your* reaction when the situation happened?

Did your child act in a way that would prevent further escalation or did their emotions get the best of them and they lashed back at the person? Understanding how your child first reacted will give you great insight into how they will perform in a stressful environment. Most children know right from wrong; however, the acid test of whether someone really "knows" is how they behave when they are tested.

Where was the teacher or authority person when the situation happened?

This question is great to ask for a number of reasons. First, you want to know if your child's natural tendency is to be positioned near a person in authority. Second, you want to know that when a situation starts to go bad, your child's reaction was to look for the teacher – or did the scenario consume their total focus. Third, you want to get a sense of how supervision is handled. All of this information is very helpful moving forward.

Now you can effectively go to work communicating with your child!

7. TEACHING YOUR CHILD AN EFFECTIVE COMMUNICATIONS STRATEGY

Physiology 70%
The way we say things 20%
What we say 10%

What your child says to all of their classmates and the people around them starts long before they ever open their mouth. Picture in your mind a sad person. You are probably envisioning someone with his shoulders sagging and his head down, maybe you see the facial expression they are carrying. Now picture someone happy. Can you see they have a different posture and breathing pattern? Their gestures are different and their face radiates their feelings.

The first place to start is with an honest assessment of how your child stands and how your child walks. Take careful note of this. Children tend to do different things with their body, depending on where they are. At home they may run all over the place, but how do they carry themselves at school? What do they look like when they are passing between classes in the hallway? Do they look like an easy target for someone looking to bully another person? This is something that has to be observed. Often a child will not know. You can help them by observing them in places that are less familiar than your home. See what their tendency is and, if it needs fixing, fix it.

What does "fix it" mean for your child? It means moving

forward so that your child becomes consciously aware of how they presenting themselves. It means walking with a confident look and feel; shoulders back, head up smiling or focused, purposeful and energetic.

Next is the specific voice quality that your child uses to communicate. Do they speak softly or assertively? Does the voice tremble with insecurity or is the tone even and certain? When your child says to someone, "Back Off" does it sound like, "BACK OFF or I'll kill you", or "Back Off because I don't want anything to do with what you are doing", or is it "Back Off because I don't want to get hurt". We all remember the tone our parents used when they meant business. Teaching your child the skills of how to use tone to send the right message to the other student is important.

First, it's what we do with our physiology; second, it's the way we say what we say and the final piece of communication is the actual words we use. Can saying the wrong words escalate a situation? *Absolutely!* It is imperative that your child uses phrases, with the correct tone and body language, to get their message across.

Here is a list of some phrases that you can practice with your child. The phrases listed are geared more toward situations in which someone may try to physically antagonize your child. However, they are great to start with because the exercise of going through this will help to anchor your child's understanding of the importance of tone and body posture.

For maximum effectiveness, practice role-playing with you being the bully and your child being the child. As you play the role (the more real you make it the better for them) "act out" what your child thinks would be a probable occurrence. Practice each phrase five times or until your child has conquered the self-consciousness that comes from "rehearsing" with mom or dad. You will find the more you do it, the better they will get at it, much the same way an actor learns to play the part of a character. Remember, for effectiveness, it is more than just the phrase; it's the body and the tone that dictate intention.

"Stop that."

"I don't want any trouble."

"Back off."

"Leave me alone."

"Don't touch me."

8. THREE EASY SKILLS YOUR CHILD MUST KNOW TO KEEP SAFE

Skill number one: Safety Zone/Danger Zone

In the practice of martial arts, many times we have the choice to be stationary and block an incoming strike or to block and move. Although as students we train for both situations, I always choose blocking and moving for the simple reason that if we attempt to block from a stationary position and strike but miss the incoming strike, we will get hit. If we form the habit of getting our body out of the way as a primary defense and then block as we move as a secondary defense, if we miss the block, our body will be out of harm's way.

In the same way, your child's first response to keeping safe should be maintaining distance from the bully. I use the terms "safety zone" and "danger zone" to make it easy to understand.

Safety zone is the distance that your child should maintain to be safe. For the purpose of bullying, safety zone is defined as a far enough distance away that the bully cannot carry on a normal conversation with your child and is out of the direct line of sight of your child. Danger zone is when this distance is broken down and the person is able to be within conversational range.

Why the distance away?

If your child maintains a 10- to 12-foot distance, it becomes inconvenient for the bully to harass them. To verbally attack your child, the bully now has to raise their voice and risk being

heard by other people standing around, and even by a teacher on duty. It's important to remember that bullies do *not* want to get caught.

When your child makes it less convenient for the person to bother them, chances are the bully will try to find someone that presents an easier target with less of a chance of getting caught.

What about confined areas like a classroom? The best application of safety zone in a classroom is to be positioned behind the attacker, a few seats back but in the same row. The reason is simple. For the bully to be able to bother your child, they have to do a complete 180-degree turn. Throwing anything at your child, giving them intimidating looks or being a nuisance in any other way becomes infinitely more difficult, especially without the teacher or other class members seeing the bullying action.

Where should my child be during lunch?

The same rule applies as with the classroom. The most optimum place to be is directly behind the person, a few tables away. This keeps throwing food or any verbal harassment minimized or completely eliminated.

What if everyone has assigned seats?

Ask your child to privately request to have their seat moved. Almost without exception, teachers and volunteers – if told in private and given good reasons for the request – will accommodate such a request. If this is not accommodated, then it is probably appropriate for the parent to make a contact with the school. Remember, neither teacher nor principal want bullying challenges at their school.

Safety and a pleasant culture that supports their goal is the best situation for everyone.

What about the playground?

Safety zone on the playground is a must! Statistics indicate that

80% of bullying behavior happens during free time. For your child to be safe, it requires awareness, not paranoia. Safety zone during free time means that your child maintain the furthest possible distance away from the bully (at least 10 to 12 feet) and that you stay at all times within that 20 to 25 feet of the teacher on duty. By doing this, your child reduces the chance of the bully being able to push, bump, kick, punch or physically harm your child.

These distance considerations also make it difficult for the bully to verbally harass your child without others hearing it or the teacher on duty being immediately aware of the situation.

Skill Number Two: Emotions in Balance

Do you think of your child as a bully? Probably not. However, when your child lashes back at the bully with a verbal, "I'm not a loser, you're a loser!" or worse, pushes and punches the bully back, then in the eyes of the principal, your child is equally to blame.

In the case of physical bullying, schools have a zero tolerance for fighting; if your child engages in it, they receive the same punishment whether they initiated it or not.

And remember this: When emotions go up, your child's ability to think clearly goes down. Defeating the bully requires strategic response, not impulsive reactions. Bullies, by their very nature, are often clever at pushing a person's emotional buttons. They can do it through overt actions or throw little annoyances that go virtually undetected by teachers. It is critical for your child's peace and happiness that they remember that their highest responsibility is to maintain self-control.

When your child allows someone else to get them angry, they forfeit control to the other person and, like a puppet on a string, the bully now controls them. By remembering that the verbal attacks are not a sign of something being wrong with your child but rather a personal defect in the other person, they will better be able to balance their emotions.

When your child's emotions get the best of them, often they will put themself in a worse situation than they were in when the offense happened. Remember: a smoldering ember often starts wildfires that can consume an entire forest. The important skill is being mentally ready to defuse the situation when it begins. When your child breaks down and examines conflict, whether on the schoolyard or between countries, it all has a starting point and oftentimes the start is something very small.

So how do you get your child skilled in this? First, let them know in advance that things like this happen. It's a great world, but it's far from perfect. There will be times that a child is "tested" and they need to be ready to deal with the situations when they happen in a calm, confident manner. Second, you should practice role-playing your child's calm response to things that may occur on the school bus, in the classroom, at lunch or during free time. By acting it out through role-play, your child will become desensitized to it and because they have practiced, when the real event occurs, they will handle it in the right way. This will prevent it from feeling like the end of the world and reacting vs. responding.

Skill Number Three: It's OK to Ask for Help

Everyone needs help from time to time. Though it's awesome to feel like you can slay the dragon on your own, often it's much easier and quicker to ask for assistance.

The game is safety and personal happiness. To get there and stay there, your child must value such feelings over the desire to handle it on their own.

Oftentimes, society feeds the myth of the "self-made" person portrayed on TV and in the press. When you have a chance to read deeper into the story, you will see that there are tremendous amounts of people who helped the "self-made" person not listed in the headlines.

In football, it's the quarterback, not the team; in baseball, often it's that pitcher or the home run hitter, not the other players who made the win possible. Even in an individual sport like golf, very rarely is the trainer or the player or the caddy given the credit for the win, it is only the winning player who gets the headlines. In business, it's names like Jobs or Gates that make the news, not the thousands of people who work day and night for a company's success. Certainly, when you look at the modern day Walt Disney movies, most are based on the hero rising up and facing an evil foe alone. All of this creates an impression that makes asking for help difficult.

It almost implies a level of deficiency or weakness for a person to admit that they don't have the answer for a challenge from a bully.

Well, if all you do is dispel the myth of needing to "go it alone," then your time reading this was well spent. When is the best time to engage help? As close to the beginning of conflict as is possible to detect. When a spouse comes home from work, it's commonplace for him or her to go through all that happened during the day, both good and bad. As a result, the person feels better and gets some clarity through feedback from their spouse.

When a child comes home and a parent asks, "How was your day?" and the child gives the standard answer, "Good", many times the parent lets it go as acceptable. As parents you may miss a phenomenal opportunity to help your child solve the inevitable challenges that will occur in a typical school day.

A parent should know the good and the bad of their child's day. A parent should be keenly aware of what their child is going through, including the challenges and how they plan to resolve problems, whether academic or social in nature. In a quest for good grades, it is important to keep in mind that emotional growth and development, including the ability to handle conflict appropriately, will determine success as much, if not more than, academic knowledge.

The second place your child needs to be aware of to ask for help is from their teacher. The key is to bring it to the teacher's attention at a private and convenient time for the teacher when the problem is first detected.

Why a private and convenient time for the teacher? It's simple courtesy. Teachers are incredibly dedicated people who have a tremendous responsibility that needs to be accomplished in a finite amount of time. They are often expected to implement more with fewer resources than what most workers at a typical company would be asked to do. They are asked to do it with 20 to 30 children (not all of whom want to be there) sitting in front of them. They have demands put on them by the school administration, by parents, and by students. Often when they comply with one group, the other group doesn't like what's being done. Remember that, although your child is the most important person in the world to you, they are one of many important people and responsibilities a teacher faces each day.

Experience has shown me, both as a teacher and from working with so many teachers over the years, that when done correctly, a teacher more often than not will be happy to accommodate your child's requests and may be able to help in ways that they haven't even thought of.

The act of courage it takes to talk to the teacher will start the learning process of making it OK to ask for help. It also provides teachers with a great "heads-up" as to what is going on in their own classrooms. Many times teachers are unaware of bullying issues that are occurring. They, like anyone else, can only focus on a couple things effectively at a time. When teaching, the focus is on what is being communicated and therefore it can be easy to miss things happening even right in the open.

Here is a simple little exercise to illustrate the point: Look around the room you are sitting in and, for fifteen seconds, notice everything that is the color green. Now close your eyes and, with your eyes closed, for fifteen seconds recall everything that is the color red. If you do the exercise, you will instantly see that though the color red is all around, you can't recall it because that's not where you put your focus.

By having your child calmly share with the teacher what has been happening and work together to figure out what can be done to help the situation, it will ensure that the best scenarios are created.

It also puts on the record that the bullying situation is occurring, so that in the future if anything happens to escalate the situation, chances are your child will be in a better position in the eyes of the school because of their proactive stance.

9. PARENT COMMUNICATION WITH THE SCHOOL

There are times when a parent needs to get involved and speak on behalf of their child.

As a teacher, nothing is more frustrating than to receive a call from an irate parent whose emotions are at a dangerously high threshold telling about how their child is being bullied.

As the conversation wears on and the drama unfolds, the parent stops for a second to catch their breath and the teacher asks, "May I ask how long has this been going on?" to which the parent responds, "Two months!!!"

The teacher thinks, "Why wasn't I told about this when it first started, two months ago?"

The parent thinks, "How could you not have known this has been going on? Aren't you paying attention to my child?"

As parents, we sometimes fall into the trap of thinking that, "I don't want to bother the teacher" or "I'm afraid if I cry wolf on something small, then if something really important happens the teacher won't take me seriously." I can tell you first-hand neither is correct. The greatest help you can give your child's teacher is to let them know through contact that you are proactively involved in your child's education.

As a teacher, the tough parents to deal with are the parents who are not known well and those who are seen only when something is wrong. It makes the teacher's job infinitely easier when steady contact is made. Think for a second about what it would be like if you were a teacher. You have 20 to 30 students to get to know and 20 to 30 sets of parents to meet and keep informed. Compare the sheer number of contacts a teacher has to make with the one contact a parent has to make – you will do them a service by keeping lines of communication open.

Read the sample letter to a teacher below. Imagine you were the teacher reading this. Wouldn't you feel appreciative that the parent took the time to write it?

Dear Mrs. Jones,

The reason for this note is that Sarah has come home for the past couple of days upset. She has told me that Jen, Olivia and Danielle have been purposely excluding her from playing at recess. I'm not sure if what Sarah says is factual or only her perspective. I wanted to give you early notice of this to see if perhaps you could check up on the situation and see if it may require intervention on your part. I know how much you value the feelings of all the students in your class. Upon examination, if there is anything I can do with Sarah to help resolve the situation, please do not hesitate to contact me.

As always I appreciate your dedication. We feel very lucky to have you as Sarah's teacher.

Sincerely,

The letter is written very carefully so that it accomplishes several goals:
- Alerts the teacher proactively at the start of potential conflict;
- Provides specifics so the teacher knows what to watch for;

• Uses the word "perception" to communicate that you realize you have only heard one side of the story;

• Acknowledges your high regard for the culture that is important to the teacher;

• Thanks the teacher for their dedication.

Contrast that approach with this phone call to the teacher:

Hi, Mrs. Jones. I am extremely upset with what I hear is going on in your classroom. Sarah has come home the past two days VERY upset as a result of the treatment she is receiving from Jen, Olivia and Danielle. I can't believe that their behavior is allowed! Now I KNOW my daughter and I KNOW she would NEVER treat anyone like that. If I don't get this resolved quickly, I'm going straight to the principal. I really thought you would be more attentive to the kids so that things like this don't happen!

This phone call accomplishes a few things as well:
• It begins with raw, negative emotions.
• It completely breaks rapport with the teacher.
• It assumes that you *KNOW* all the facts.
• It is accusatory to the other children and at the same time doesn't consider that Sarah may have done something to create this.
• It expresses disappointment and makes generalizations about the care provided at the school.
• It threatens.
• It insults.

The approach you take with the teacher can make or break the quality of your child's school year. If treated fairly and with respect, your child's teacher can be an incredible asset. Proceed with courtesy and care!

10. COMMUNICATING WITH
THE BULLY'S PARENTS

At times it's probably appropriate to have a conversation with the parents of the bully.

In many cases, your child's mistreatment is probably a secret to the bully's parents. I feel certain in assuming that the bully is not going home to his mom at day's end and saying, "Hey mom, guess what? I teased Tommy all day long! Aren't you proud of me?"

Though it's no fun hearing that your child engaged in bullying behavior, it's always better to find out than to have your child learn inappropriate habits and suffer the inevitable consequences that come with treating people poorly.

As in the teacher's dialogue from the previous pages and maybe even more so, **PROCEED WITH CAUTION AND CARING.** Also, be fully aware that you may quickly understand from whom the bullying child has learned their destructive behavior. If this is the outcome, you need to employ another strategy. But be careful not to assume in advance this will be the outcome. Many times, it's not.

Here is a sample phone dialogue:

Hi Sandy, this is Julie Reilly, Sarah's mom. Our kids are in Mrs. Jones' class together. The reason for my call is there seems to be a challenge at recess and I was hoping I could discuss this with you to see if, together, *we can figure something out.*

For the past couple days my daughter, Sarah, has come home a little upset. She told me that your daughter, Jen, as well as Olivia and Danielle, have purposely excluded her from playing at recess. I'm not sure if what Sarah is telling me is factual or merely her perspective. May I ask: Has your daughter mentioned anything about what's been going on at recess?

Perhaps you could have a conversation with Jen to get her perspective on what's happening. If it is something that Sarah is doing that's causing your daughter to feel badly, I want to make sure that I address it with her so that she stops the behavior immediately. I'm sure that whatever it is, working together we can get this resolved. Our kids are going to be in school together for a long time and I want to make sure that they enjoy each other's company. I appreciate your taking the time to look into this.

This brief phone conversation accomplishes multiple goals:

• It takes the time in the beginning to create a little rapport with the other parent;

• It maintains a non-accusatory tone;

• It alerts the parent of a challenge that is happening, in most cases without their knowledge;

• It promotes a discovery of the specifics of the situation;

• It uses the word "perception" to communicate that you realize you have only heard one side of the story;

• It acknowledges that *your* child may be part of problem;

• And it thanks the other parent for investigating on your behalf.

11. FREQUENTLY ASKED QUESTIONS

When is it OK to fight?

Replace the word "fight" with the phrase "defend myself." The only time it is OK to defend oneself is when your child is put into a situation where they are being physically threatened, they cannot get away and there is no adult supervision able or willing to prevent trouble. The likelihood of that happening in school or on the bus is slim.

It's my experience that 99% of conflict starts with verbal or psychological tactics. By sharpening your child's ability to use the tools outlined, more than likely your child will never have to resort to using physical skills. The same rules apply to adults as they do to children.

My child is afraid to tell a teacher because they don't want to be called a tattletale. What should I do?

Educate your child in the differences between being a tattletale and reporting bullying behavior. It's important for children to understand that tattling occurs when you are purposefully telling on someone for the sole purpose of getting them in trouble.

Reporting bullying behavior is a smart strategy that is used to stop conflict before it escalates. Its purpose is to keep your child safe, not for the pleasure of seeing someone get in trouble.

My child was told that if they reported the behavior to the teacher, they would be in for even worse bullying. What do I tell my child?

Tell your child that **bullies DO NOT want to get caught** and, as a result, they will often threaten and use words like tattling as a way of making it appear not cool. This is common. What is not common is for a bully to continue to pursue someone they know will report them. A little courage in the beginning will pay off in big gains in your child's happiness for the rest of the year. Your child will find the bully will migrate away from them and toward someone who will be an easier target to pursue.

How do I know if my child is not bringing these problems on themself?

Communication is the key: communication with your child, communication with the teacher and communication with the other parents. It's important that you keep informed. Ask your child questions beyond, "How was school?" Probe to see how they speak to others and how they react to situations. When they share something that happened in their day, follow up with specific questions that will reveal their behaviors and perceptions of events.

When meeting with teachers, ask questions beyond academics. Include questions such as, "How does my daughter do socializing with other children?" or "Have you noticed any social situations that my son may need to handle better?" As a parent you need to gain insight into how your child behaves when you're not around.

When you speak with other parents or attend a function where parents will be, be sure to listen twice as much as you talk. This is a great opportunity to hear other perceptions that are floating around the parentsphere. It may give you information that you can later gently bring up to your child.

What if my child is being picked on by a group of bullies?

Every group is made up of individuals. The first defense is to get your child into a peer group. By not being alone, it makes them less likely to be a target. The second defense is how your child carries themself; make certain that they practice the habits covered in the earlier chapters for projecting confidence. Third, be sure that they are not doing anything to either make the situation worse, such as either fighting back or playing the victim role.

My child is by nature shy and quiet, does this make them more of a target?

No! What makes your child a target is trying to become a superhero and fight off the bully with strong physical skills or verbal judo. Your child becomes protected when they learn a skill set to avoid conflict or to know what to do when conflict arises. Many children possess introvert tendencies. The good news is they don't have to change; you simply need to add a degree of depth to their understanding of conflict and how to handle it.

My child has continually tried to ignore the bully, but the person continues to torment them. What should I do?

While there are situations when ignoring a bullying behavior may be the right response, as a long-term strategy for dealing with continual harassment, it falls short. Ignoring has been shown to work best for small first-time occurrences. Ignoring, by itself as a long-term strategy, may be making the situation worse. Take action, evaluate the situation and make a better choice.

Girls are bullying my son. What do I tell him to do?

Most situations your son will find himself in will be psychological and not physical. Whether it's a girl, a boy, someone smaller or younger, bullying behavior is bullying behavior and your son needs to handle the situation appropriately by applying the strategies in this guide.

I'm not sure if the children in my daughter's class are bullies, but I do know that my child doesn't feel good about herself when she is at school. What should I do?

Understand that with children many times they don't even realize that their actions are causing anyone sadness. Many times they are simply caught up in the games or activities they are in and don't appreciate that, by repeatedly excluding someone, they engage in bullying behavior. A quick fix to this could be a simple note to the teacher *(see the sample note in the previous chapter)*. A teacher with professional sensitivity can integrate your child into the group and also teach the children that have been causing the exclusion to be more sensitive to others that may want to play.

My child has trouble making friends. How can I help?

Teach your child to be a friend instead of trying to find a friend. When your child is kind, helpful and courteous to all classmates, friendships will naturally happen. Just be sure to curb your child's expectations. It may not happen immediately, but consistency over time will win out. At times, children try to demand that people be their friends and just like in the adult world, it just doesn't work that way.

I'm worried that the situation has blown up and may be heading to physical confrontation. What should I do?

Any time that a situation has quickly deteriorated or you find out about something too late, take immediate action by communicating with the teacher and the principal. Remember, you are not an annoyance to them; you are helping them by giving them vital communications and information. Though no one likes these problems happening at their school, each would much rather know now than find out after a physical confrontation.

Will enrolling my child in karate classes diminish their getting bullied?

It depends on the school that you enroll them in. If the school's teachers approach conflict from both a psychological and physical context, then there may be great value in your child's ability to handle the most common situations that arise. If the school focuses exclusively on physical self-defense, while good if a physical altercation occurs, it will do nothing for the 97% of the common situations that arise in a typical grade school.

My spouse and I disagree on how our child should handle the bullying situation that they are dealing with. What should we do?

Agree to continue to communicate until you both find an alternative that meets both of your needs. To get off the immediacy of the specific emotional situation that your child is confronted with, a good question to ask is: "If my child was an adult and this situation was happening at work, how would we want them to handle it?"

Questions like this apply long-term thinking that can be helpful in reducing heightened emotions that are often associated with significantly different opinions among spouses.

I'm dealing with a teacher who believes bullying is just part of growing up and is not being responsive to my needs. What should I do?

While conflict (another word for bullying) will naturally occur for the rest of your and your child's life, it should not imply that your child should be destined to endure poor treatment. When others around your child aren't as helpful as you feel they should be, it just puts the responsibility on your child to be even more aware of the strategies outlined in the previous chapters.

For extreme negligence, or repeated lack of sensitivity to your needs, it may also be helpful to set up a meeting with a guidance counselor or the principal to share your concerns.

A child who has their own extreme emotional challenges is bullying my child and I believe their bullying behavior is tolerated because of the disability. How do I handle this?

When a child with varying special needs is integrated into a classroom, it can be a great experience for your child. It can afford the opportunity for your child to develop compassion and understanding and a greater appreciation for their own abilities that, at times, are probably taken for granted. However, when a child's deficiencies adversely affect the quality of the classroom and/or through specific bullying behavior continually causes your child's experience to be interrupted, for both your child's sake and for the sake of the special needs student, this needs be addressed immediately by the school; the present situation with its hoped for noble outcome is not working.

12. FINAL THOUGHTS
AND ADDITIONAL RESOURCES

One is the loneliest number.

For both child and parents, not knowing what to do about bullying can be scary. What's the solution? Make sure you surround yourself with a great team of advisors who have been in your shoes and understand your unique needs. For your children it is surrounding themselves with a positive peer group and role models that set an example of leadership and an expectation that motivates your child to take the right action no matter the situation.

Within every challenge is the opportunity for a greater level of growth and development… and dealing with a bully is no different. Addressing it appropriately while it is small strengthens courage, communication and develops a strong sense of confidence and self-esteem. This guide will give you a solid start on your journey in navigating the sometime tricky waters of raising a child. For some, this resource may be sufficient and if so, mission accomplished – congratulations! The book will be a continual resource for you to reference.

Others may seek additional resources to spur your child's full growth potential. If this is you, please consider one or all of the options below. Whichever camp you find yourself in, please know that I wish you and your family well and that no matter how life challenges you or your children, with the right mindset and strategy you will be victorious every time.

DONE WITH BULLYING SEMINAR

This is the perfect complement to reading this book.

To learn the dates of the next **Done With Bullying**™ seminar please email Info@PersonalBestKarate.com. These age-appropriate classes will cover the most probable situations and provide easy solutions to keep your child and their classmates safe. Clarity creates power! In this seminar your child will learn to articulate in 10 seconds or less exactly what to do if they are bullied… GUARANTEED!!!

GET YOUR CHILD ON THEIR PERSONAL BEST PATH

If you would give your child the gift of a FREE trial in our award winning character based martial arts program that will reinforce family value and teach mental and physical skills to ensure they are safe Please go to www.PersonalBestKarate.com.

We promise that our team of highly skilled martial arts teachers and mentors will help you and your family feel right at home.

ABOUT THE AUTHOR
CHRISTOPHER M. RAPPOLD

Christopher Rappold is a master teacher, trainer and blogger who has been working with children and families for more than 25 years. He has presented bullying programs to more than 30 school districts and is a widely recognized expert at presenting safety strategies and bullying prevention in layman's terms while also filling gaps left by educating and involving teachers, parents and school administrators.

Rappold is the founder of Personal Best Karate, martial arts schools presently located in New England, and serves as both an owner and president of the franchise. His form of teaching honors the potential of each student's individual capabilities and works to ensure just the right level of challenge is presented so that the student can maintain sustained and lasting growth and improvement.

Rappold has been a member of Team Paul Mitchell (the top-rated sport karate team in the world) dating back to 1988 and currently serves as the team's Executive Director. Rappold has also won the W.A.K.O. World Championship in three different weight divisions.

For **Done With Bullying**™ information or to schedule a program for your school or group, please call (508) 285-5425 or email Info@PersonalBestKarate.com.

CPSIA information can be obtained
at www.ICGtesting.com
Printed in the USA
LVHW091616160320
650181LV00001B/442

9 781519 423528